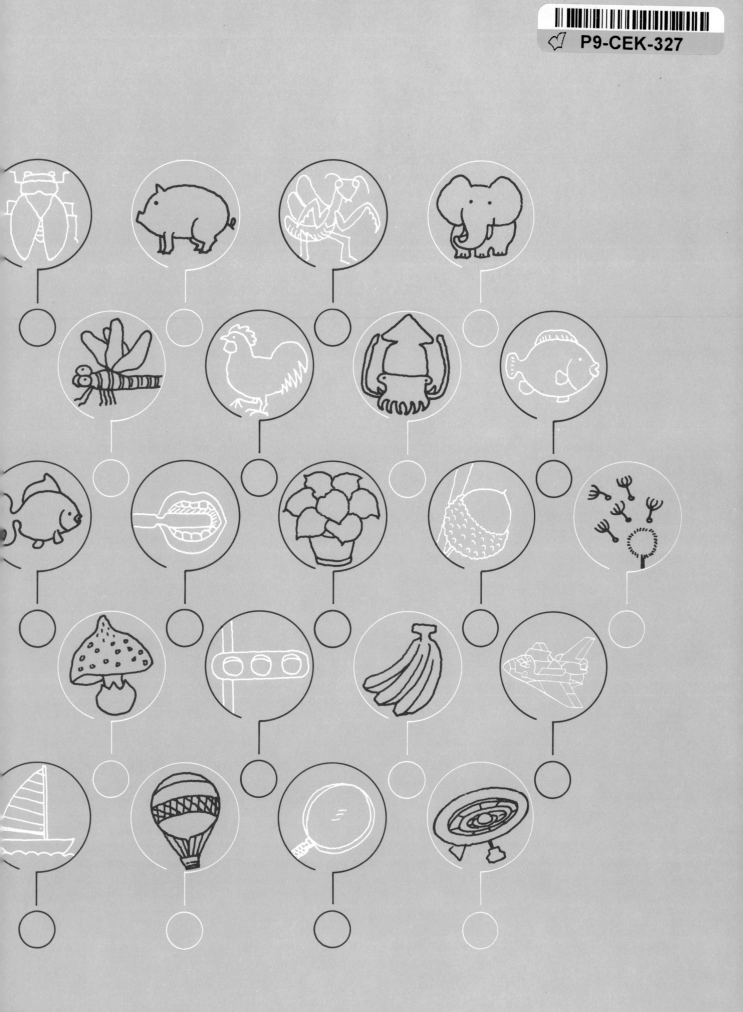

A Child's First Library of Learning

Explorers & Adventurers

TIME-LIFE BOOKS • ALEXANDRIA, VIRGINIA

Contents

Why Do People Explore?

ANSWER The first explorers were driven by curiosity and the need to find food and fuel. Later explorers left home to trade for goods they did not have, or to conquer new territory, or to try to convert others to their religion. Today, people find it exciting to visit remote areas like high, icy mountains or thick, leafy jungles.

1. Early humans

Most early explorers were looking for food when they found new lands.

2. Vikings

The Vikings traded goods with Persia in the east, and discovered a new continent to the west.

3. Caravans

Merchants used camel caravans to carry the spices, jewels, and cloth they traded.

4. Conquistadors

Spanish adventurers often forced their own way of life on the new lands and peoples they found.

▲ 6. A polar express

Dogsleds carried explorers who wanted to be the first to reach the North Pole or the South Pole.

▲ 5. Wonder why we wander?

Many explorers left home simply because they were curious about what they would find. They discovered fabulous plants and animals in faraway places.

▲ 7. King of the mountain

Modern adventurers like the thrill of reaching a place that no one has visited before, or getting to old places in new ways.

◄ 8. Up and away

Today's explorers are using some of yesterday's tools—such as the hot-air balloon—to set distance records.

▼ 9. Out of this world

Looking for new places to explore, humans have traveled into space. What do you think we will find on other planets?

● To the Parent

Curiosity and the need to find food kept early peoples on the move, whereas later societies were driven to explore by economic or religious motives. Current adventurers are pushing the limits of technology—and expanding the boundaries of scientific knowledge—as they try alternative methods of exploration.

❓ How Did Early Explorers Travel?

ANSWER The first explorers went everywhere on foot. Later on, they used pack animals such as horses, camels, and donkeys to carry their supplies—and themselves! Ancient peoples also paddled simple boats. Once they learned to use wind power, they sailed long distances.

■ By foot

▲ Early peoples explored their world on foot. Some carried everything they needed for an expedition in backpacks like these.

■ On horseback

By using horses to carry goods, early explorers were able to go farther and faster, and to bring more with them for trading.

■ Over the water

► People power

The earliest boats were rafts made of logs. People poled or paddled the raft to travel in the direction they wanted to go.

► Wind power

The ancient Mesopotamians and Egyptians put sails on boats made of reeds. The wind drove the boats faster and farther than humans could row them.

◄ Naval powers

European sailing ships like this one crossed the oceans carrying soldiers and their supplies. The soldiers used their weapons to conquer other lands.

● To the Parent

The duration of an expedition has always been limited by the supplies its members can bring with them. Early humans met their needs for food, shelter, and clothing as they went, but later explorers provisioned themselves in advance. By the late 16th century, explorers had succeeded in traveling around the world in full-rigged ships.

❓ What Equipment Do Explorers Need?

ANSWER All explorers need methods of finding their way to distant places and getting back home. Their navigational instruments have ranged from a simple compass to a complex computer. Explorers also need a means of travel, some food to eat along the way, and shelter to protect them from wind, rain, and wild animals.

▲ A keen pair of eyes
The position of stars in the sky guided early explorers on their journeys. Marker stars, like the North Star, do not move much.

A cross-staff
The cross-staff, developed about 1500, gave a ship's latitude, or distance from the equator. To use it, a sailor lined up one end of the shorter stick with the Sun or the North Star and the other end with the horizon.

▶ A sextant
The sextant was much more accurate than the cross-staff. It came into use around 1730. Two mirrors and an eyepiece showed the angle of the sun above the horizon, and thus the ship's latitude. Its name comes from the curved scale at the base, which is one-sixth of a circle.

▶ A trusty map

The first map ever drawn was probably just a few lines scratched in the dust. By the time of Columbus, maps were drawn on parchment or printed on paper, and they looked like this. You can now find a map of every place on Earth and under the sea—and even some parts of space!

▼ A place to eat and sleep

Tents have sheltered explorers from the earliest days. Whether made of animal skins or space-age fabric, a tent can be set up almost anywhere, and it is easy to carry.

TRY THIS!

■ Find the polestar

Go outside on a clear night, face north, and look at the Big Dipper. Imagine a line running up through the two stars on the right side of the "dipper." The next big bright star the line hits is the polestar (or North Star), which stays fixed above the North Pole.

● To the Parent

Like all explorers, children are reassured by the thought that they can find home again after ranging far afield. You can spur their interest in geography by helping them draw a map of their neighborhood. Older children can plot routes or serve as "copilots" on family trips.

❓ Can People Cross the Ocean in Canoes?

ANSWER The people who settled the islands of the Pacific (the largest ocean in the world) sailed across the water in canoes that were 60 to 100 feet long. Each canoe was made of two hulls fastened together, with a tall sail rising from the deck between them. The canoes carried up to 100 people, so they also had plenty of paddle power!

■ Where they went

Some experts believe that the Pacific Islanders first came from Asia. They sailed east from island to island. Many roamed north to Hawaii, while others went southeast to Easter Island.

■ What they took with them

▲ Livestock
The seafarers brought chickens, pigs, and enough food to feed the animals until the canoe reached a new island.

▲ Seeds of a new life
The voyagers carried breadfruit *(above),* coconuts, taros, and bananas to grow on their new islands.

■ How they found their way

Pacific sailors got from one island to another using maps made of wood. Each stick in the map stood for an ocean current or a sailing route. Shells or stones showed the location of islands.

▲ Hooked on travel
Hooks like this one, from New Zealand, caught big fish or sharks at sea.

● To the Parent

The first travelers in Oceania made short hops from one island to the next, hugging the coast. Later they undertook longer passages from one island group to another. Months were spent in preparation for a voyage. Family groups, tools, and supplies all had to be chosen with care to establish a new settlement far from the home islands.

? Who Were the Vikings?

ANSWER The Vikings were adventurers who sailed from Norway, Sweden, and Denmark about 1,000 years ago. They conquered parts of England and France. Vikings discovered and settled Iceland, then visited Greenland and Newfoundland hundreds of years before other Europeans. Vikings used open wooden boats with sails and oars. Traveling up rivers and over land, they traded with Russia and Persia.

■ A Viking ship

For ocean voyages, the Vikings built boats that were as long as three school buses. They nailed narrow boards onto a wooden frame, then sealed the boards with pitch (a waterproof tar made from pine trees).

■ It's moo-ving day!

The Vikings took their families and farm animals with them to new lands. At sea, everyone lived in the open area in the boat's center.

■ Settling in

The Vikings built houses of stone and sod. Parts of these houses can still be seen today, proof that the Vikings landed in North America.

Some Viking leaders were women. Freydis, daughter of Erik the Red, led a Viking expedition to the New World around AD 1000.

❓ Where Did Marco Polo Go?

ANSWER Marco Polo was 17 when he left Venice to go to China with his father and uncle in 1271. It took them nearly four years to reach Beijing, where Marco met the emperor, Kublai Khan. After traveling all over Asia as a reporter for the khan, Marco returned to Venice in 1295 and told of the wonders he had seen. Many people thought he was making up such marvels as coal, porcelain, and paper money.

▲ **Emperor Kublai Khan**

▶ **Across Asia by caravan**
Marco Polo used a caravan of horses and camels to cross the Gobi Desert. On this part of the journey, it took the travelers one month to go 380 miles.

▲ **Coins for cloth**
Europeans treasured silk but did not know how to make it. They gave Chinese merchants gold, silver, and horses in exchange for the precious cloth.

14

▲ A car fit for a khan

Kublai Khan sometimes rode in a pavilion carried by several elephants. Marco Polo told of this and other sights in a book about his travels.

▲ The greatest palace that ever was

Marco Polo was amazed by the size of Kublai Khan's palace in Beijing. The wall around it was four miles long and "a good 10 paces in height."

◀ A land of lighter dough

The Polos were surprised to find that pieces of paper, not coins of gold, were used as money in China.

● To the Parent

Marco Polo was probably not the first European to visit China, but he was the first to describe it at length back home. A recent study claims he never went at all but cobbled together tales told by others. Traveler or not, Polo inspired many people—including Columbus—to venture into foreign lands.

Who Was Ibn Battuta?

ANSWER Ibn Battuta of Morocco made a pilgrimage, or religious journey, to the Muslim holy city of Mecca in 1325. He then decided to visit every country in the world that had a large Muslim community. Ibn Battuta spent almost 30 years traveling. He tried never to use the same road twice!

Ibn Battuta traveled 75,000 miles, equal to circling Earth three times.

■ The world tour, 1333

Wherever he went, Ibn Battuta took his wives, his children, and his servants. Moving about two miles per hour, the caravan crossed the desert at night to escape the heat of day.

■ Marvelous mud

Ibn Battuta may have visited this beautiful mosque when he crossed the Sahara to reach the kingdom of Mali, West Africa, in 1352. Built of mud many centuries ago, it has survived because thousands of people repair it by hand at the end of each rainy season.

■ The balance of trade

In an open-air market such as this one, Ibn Battuta could have traded gold from tropical West Africa for sugar, cloth, pepper, or salt. The items for sale in the market were brought by boat or camel caravan from countries all across the Arab world.

■ One hump or two?

Caravans of up to 400 camels still cross the deserts of Africa today. The animals carry salt from mines in Mali. One camel can carry food and water to last a person 40 days.

? How Did Chinese Explorers Travel?

ANSWER After the Great Wall of China was built in 300 BC, most emperors did not allow the Chinese to leave the country. But in 1405, a new emperor put a man named Cheng Ho in charge of 317 ships with a crew of 27,000 men. Cheng Ho sailed first to India. Later he sailed around the tip of Africa—60 years before the first Europeans.

▲ **Pointing the way home**

A magnetic compass like this one was in use in China by 1100. It helped Chinese sailors find their way at sea.

European ship

■ **Chinese treasure ship**

The ships that Columbus sailed across the Atlantic to America were puny compared with Cheng Ho's ships, which were 10 times heavier and as long as a football field.

■ Chinese sea chart

The Chinese made the first printed maps. This chart, made after Cheng Ho's voyages, shows India at the top and Africa at the bottom (it is not drawn to scale). It tells sailors how to get from port to port.

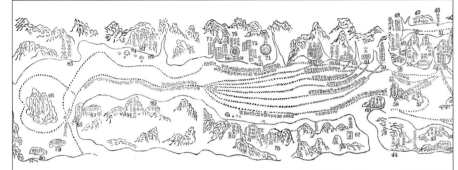

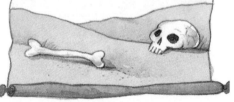

"In this desert there are winds that kill all who encounter them. So far as the eye can reach, the route is marked out by the bleached bones of men who have perished in the attempt to cross the desert."

—Fa-hsien, a Chinese Buddhist monk who crossed the Gobi on his way to India in AD 399

◀ **Treasures from the west**

Cheng Ho returned to China with treasure ships loaded with gifts for the emperor: leopards, giraffes, gemstones, and magnifying glasses. The giraffes were thought to bring luck.

● To the Parent

Two years after Cheng Ho returned to China, his sponsor, the last Ming emperor Ch'eng-tsu, died. The new dynasty was indifferent to foreign trade, so the treasure fleet was disbanded. With it went China's tradition of exploration. Indeed, reports of early Chinese expeditions in the Pacific—including a possible discovery of Australia—were buried.

Who Was Vasco da Gama?

ANSWER European sailors of the Middle Ages were afraid to travel too far from home for many reasons. They believed that monsters lay in wait for them beyond the edges of the known world. The sailors got nervous when they crossed the equator because the stars that had always guided their way home were in different positions. Portuguese explorer Vasco da Gama tried to overcome the men's fears and find a sea route to the spice trade of India.

▼ Into the unknown
Early explorers hugged the coast of Africa as they sailed south, but in 1497 Vasco da Gama tried a new way. To catch the best winds and currents, he sailed out of sight of land and far into the Atlantic Ocean.

▶ Da Gama was here!
When da Gama landed on the coast of Africa, he set up a pillar topped by a cross to claim the land for Portugal. As he sailed away, the local people pulled the pillar down.

■ Vasco da Gama

Da Gama became a rich man after he found a sea route to India. The king of Portugal gave him 1,000 gold coins a year, as well as a town to rule and the title Viceroy of India.

"Many of our men fell ill, their feet and hands swelling, and their gums growing over their teeth so they could not eat."

—Sailor's diary from the da Gama voyage

▲ Your spices or your life!

Da Gama attacked Arab merchant ships that did not want to give up their spice trade with India. The Portuguese ships carried 20 cannons, the most powerful weapons in the Indian Ocean at the time.

● To the Parent

Tedium, spoiled food, scurvy, and the fear of never returning home were just some of the hazards of 15th-century ocean voyages. As the Portuguese ventured east, they also met armed resistance from Arab merchants who held spice-trade monopolies. Da Gama's success in overcoming these difficulties was more highly regarded at the time than the discoveries of Columbus.

❓ Who Discovered America?

(ANSWER) Asiatic hunters walked across dry land to the western tip of Alaska during the Ice Ages, some 20,000 years ago. They were the first people to find America. Vikings left stones in Canada around AD 1000, proving they landed there. Christopher Columbus explored islands in the Caribbean and part of Central America during four voyages of discovery from 1492 to 1502.

■ Ice Age discoverers

■ St. Brendan

Some people think an Irish priest named St. Brendan may have discovered America about 1,000 years before Columbus. In 1976 and 1977, Tim Severin *(left)* sailed this old-style boat from Ireland to Newfoundland, Canada, to show that St. Brendan could have done it.

■ The Vikings

The first signs of European explorers in America are the ruins of stone huts built by Vikings in Newfoundland around AD 1000. The Vikings called this place "Vinland" because so many grapevines grew there.

■ Columbus

Trying to find a new route to the silk and spices of China and Japan, Christopher Columbus sailed west from Spain with three ships: the *Niña,* the *Pinta,* and the *Santa María.* On October 12, 1492, he landed on Watling Island in the Bahamas.

● To the Parent

Claims have been made (but not proved) that African, Chinese, or Welsh explorers found America before Columbus. Greek philosophers of the fourth century BC established that Earth is a sphere, but Columbus was the first to put the knowledge to practical use: His sea road to the West Indies introduced Europeans to a new continent.

What Did Magellan Do?

ANSWER In 1519, Ferdinand Magellan left Spain with a fleet of five ships carrying 237 men. The fleet sailed around the world—the first time anyone had done so. But when it returned in 1522, only one ship and 18 men were left. The others had died or deserted along the way. Magellan himself was killed by islanders in the Philippines.

"We went three months and 20 days without getting any kind of fresh food. We ate biscuit which was biscuit no longer but a powder full of worms. We also had to use sawdust for food, and for rats we paid half a ducat apiece."

—Antonio Pigafetta, one of Magellan's crew

■ Finding a way through

Philippines

Spain

The Magellan expedition took the route shown here to sail around the world from 1519 to 1522. The solid line is the part of the voyage Magellan completed.

■ Odd fellows

Magellan's men were amazed by the strange animals they found in South America and the Pacific Ocean. They called penguins "geese" and seals "sea wolves."

▲ Penguins

► Flying fish

▲ Vicunas

◄ A solo voyage

Sixteen-year-old Robin Graham uses a sextant to find his position at sea during his sailing trip around the world—alone! "I knew exactly where I was," he said, "even though I could not see any land." The journey took 1,739 days—from July 27, 1965 to April 20, 1970—and covered 30,600 miles.

● To the Parent

Magellan's expedition proved that Columbus had been correct in trying to reach the East Indies by sailing west from Europe. Spanish traders made a tidy profit from the cargo of cloves that the surviving ship brought home. Magellan's passage from the Atlantic to the Pacific, the Strait of Magellan, remained a key shipping route until the Panama Canal opened in 1914.

Who Was Esteban?

ANSWER Esteban was a slave brought to America in 1528. On a voyage with Spanish explorer Cabeza de Vaca, he was captured by Indians but escaped and made his way to Mexico City. As he traveled, Esteban learned all about the territory and its native people. The Spanish sent him out again to look for the legendary Golden Cities, which were never found.

Esteban's travels

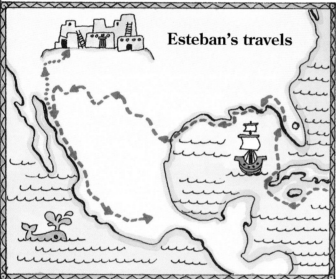

1. Esteban is captured

Esteban was traveling with Spanish explorers when their ship wrecked on an island near Texas. Indians living on the island took Esteban prisoner.

2. He gets away

Esteban and three of the explorers escaped from the Indians. It took the men two years to reach a Spanish settlement in Mexico.

Scholars believe the fabled Golden Cities may have been a Zuni pueblo called Hawaikuh. The houses shone gold in the light of the setting sun.

▲ 5. He gets the royal treatment

As he traveled west, Esteban was honored with gifts of turquoise and other precious items by the Indians he met.

▲ 4. Esteban leads the way

From Mexico City, Esteban set off as a scout in advance of a party of Spanish explorers. A priest led the group that followed.

▲ 3. He makes new friends

During his travels, Esteban learned to speak six Indian languages. He also came to know the plants, the animals, and the customs of the land.

● **To the Parent**

Esteban's story has a sad ending: He was killed by Pueblo Indians, and his companions returned to Mexico. The Spanish continued their quest for the Golden Cities, however. In 1540, they dispatched a force of 225 horsemen, 60 soldiers, and 1,300 Indians to find the storied site. Although no gold turned up, the party did find the Rio Grande and the Grand Canyon.

What Did Real Pirates Do?

(ANSWER) Pirates attacked sailing ships and stole their cargo. When Spain began sending ships full of gold and silver back to Europe from the New World, pirates from other nations waited along the way and took the treasure. The crews tried to defend their ships, but pirates were ruthless fighters. They often killed the sailors and set the ships on fire.

■ A boarding party

Armed to the teeth, pirates climb aboard a treasure ship to fight its crew. Many sailors joined gangs of pirates to avoid being killed or left behind on a sinking ship.

■ Pirate flags

The skull and crossbones of the Jolly Roger *(right)* flew from the mast of many pirate ships. The flag sent a grim message to other vessels: Give up—or else! Other pirate captains flew their own personal flags, some of which are shown here.

▼ Calico Jack Rackham

▼ Thomas Tew

▼ Christopher Condent

▼ Emmanuel Wynne

▼ Blackbeard

Anne Bonny and Mary Read

Henry Morgan

Blackbeard (Edward Teach)

● **To the Parent**

Legendary pirates appeal to the imagination, but real pirates were nautical criminals. Some were women; others—including Sir Francis Drake—were government agents sent to attack foreign shipping. A few reformed after their buccaneering lives. Henry Morgan, for example, was knighted and became deputy governor of Jamaica.

What Was the "Great Southern Continent"?

ANSWER Until about 250 years ago, people in northern countries did not know what the world looked like in the far south. Some thought that it must be covered with a huge piece of land. Otherwise, they said, the weight of the land in the north would make the planet tip over!

■ The unknown land

In 1570, a German mapmaker drew a new map of the world. In the south, he showed a big chunk of land. He called it "Terra Australis Nondum Cognita," which means "Not-Yet-Known Southern Land." The explorer Captain Cook sailed out to find this land.

Terra Australis Nondum Cognita

■ Captain Cook

James Cook, one of the most famous explorers in history, was born a poor boy in England in 1728. Cook was smart and stubborn. He taught himself navigation so that he could become a ship's captain.

What are *those* things?

On its first trip to the South Seas, Cook's ship landed on the shores of Australia. There the sailors saw kangaroos for the first time.

Sandwich Islands

On his third voyage to the Pacific Ocean, Cook found some islands that were not on any map. He called them the "Sandwich Islands" after the Earl of Sandwich. Today we know them as the Hawaiian Islands.

Nice and icy

On their second trip south, Cook and his men saw icebergs, which they called "islands of ice," near Antarctica. Cook's sailors chipped off blocks of ice and melted them for fresh drinking water.

● **To the Parent**

In three far-flung voyages between 1768 and 1778, Captain James Cook mapped much of the Pacific Ocean, including Tahiti, Easter Island, New Zealand, the Hawaiian Islands, and the east coast of Australia. His travels near Antarctica disproved the notion that the Southern Hemisphere contained one huge continent.

❓ Who Were Lewis and Clark?

ANSWER In 1804, President Thomas Jefferson asked Meriwether Lewis and William Clark to find a way across the American west. For two years, the explorers and their companions crossed unknown mountains and paddled down dangerous rivers. Finally, on November 12, 1806, they reached the Pacific Ocean.

Lewis & Clark's Route

Outbound ⟵

Return ⇠ ⇢

■ The way west

With the help of Indian people they met along the way, Lewis and Clark mapped a route from the Mississippi River to the Pacific Ocean.

■ Bears and bugs

Grizzly bears sometimes chased Lewis and Clark's men up trees. But the creatures that bugged them the most were hungry mosquitoes.

"Musquetoes extreemly troublesome...my dog even howls with the torture...they are so numerous that we frequently get them in our throats as we breath." —from the journal of William Clark, July 1806

■ Two heroes

Many people aided Lewis and Clark in finding their way to the Pacific. Two people—York and Sacagawea—were especially helpful.

▼ All about York

York was William Clark's slave. He was very brave, and an expert at canoeing. The Indians were fascinated by York. Some tried to rub the color from his skin.

▲ All about Sacagawea

A 16-year-old Shoshone woman named Sacagawea traveled with Lewis and Clark as a guide. She helped them make friends with Indians along the way.

● To the Parent

The United States doubled in size when Thomas Jefferson purchased the Louisiana Territory from the French in 1803. Lewis and Clark's expedition blazed trails from St. Louis, Missouri, to the mouth of the Columbia River between present-day Oregon and Washington, opening the West to settlement.

Do Explorers Ever Get Lost?

ANSWER Some explorers set out to find one country but find another one instead. Other explorers simply get lost. Several important discoveries have been made by explorers who went astray.

■ You mean this isn't China?

John Cabot, an Italian explorer, sailed from England in 1498 in search of China. Instead, he landed on the coast of Canada. When Cabot got back, he said he had found the court of the Chinese rulers.

CHINA

■ You mean this isn't India?

Pedro Cabral was a Portuguese explorer who went looking for a new route to India in 1500. But he sailed too far west and landed on the coast of Brazil. Cabral then claimed the land for Portugal.

INDIA

■ Dr. Livingstone, I presume?

David Livingstone, a Scottish doctor, went to Africa in 1841, hoping to expose the slave trade and put an end to it. Many years later, Livingstone became ill and got lost. An American newspaper reporter, Henry Stanley, found Livingstone, sick and weak, in the village of Ujiji in present-day Tanzania.

MINI-DATA

■ A really long shopping trip

When Christopher Columbus went to America in 1492, he was looking for China, with its spices and gold. Instead, the "New World" gave Europe new foods, including turkeys, corn, tomatoes, pineapples, peanuts, potatoes, and avocados.

● **To the Parent**

Many of the first Europeans to reach the New World were looking for Asia, the source of rich spices—and, legend had it, jewels and gold. But overland routes to Asia were dangerous, so the rulers of England, Spain, and Portugal financed voyages west—such as those of Christopher Columbus and John Cabot—to find an ocean passage.

? Who Was Mary Kingsley?

ANSWER Mary Kingsley was an Englishwoman who explored West Africa in the late 1800s. She found out many new things about the people and animals who lived there. Kingsley loved adventure. She wrote some funny and exciting books about her travels.

■ Saved by a skirt

Even in the hottest parts of Africa, Mary Kingsley wore long sleeves, a long skirt, and thick petticoats. One day, while walking along a path, she fell into an elephant pit filled with long, sharp stakes. "It is at times like these you realise the blessings of a good thick skirt," she said. The cloth protected her, so she was only bruised.

■ Crocodiles beware!

Mary Kingsley traveled a lot by canoe. One time, she wrote, a crocodile "chose to get his front paws over the stern of my canoe." Kingsley hit him on the nose with her paddle to make him go away.

■ Climb every mountain

Even though the weather was stormy, Mary Kingsley climbed to the top of Mt. Cameroon, the tallest mountain in West Africa. There she left a card with her name on it.

● To the Parent

Mary Kingsley was an independent Victorian woman who took to exploration after a youth spent caring for her parents. She wrote several popular books about the animals and people of West Africa, particularly a cannibal tribe called the Fang. Kingsley died of fever while serving as a nurse in the Boer War in South Africa.

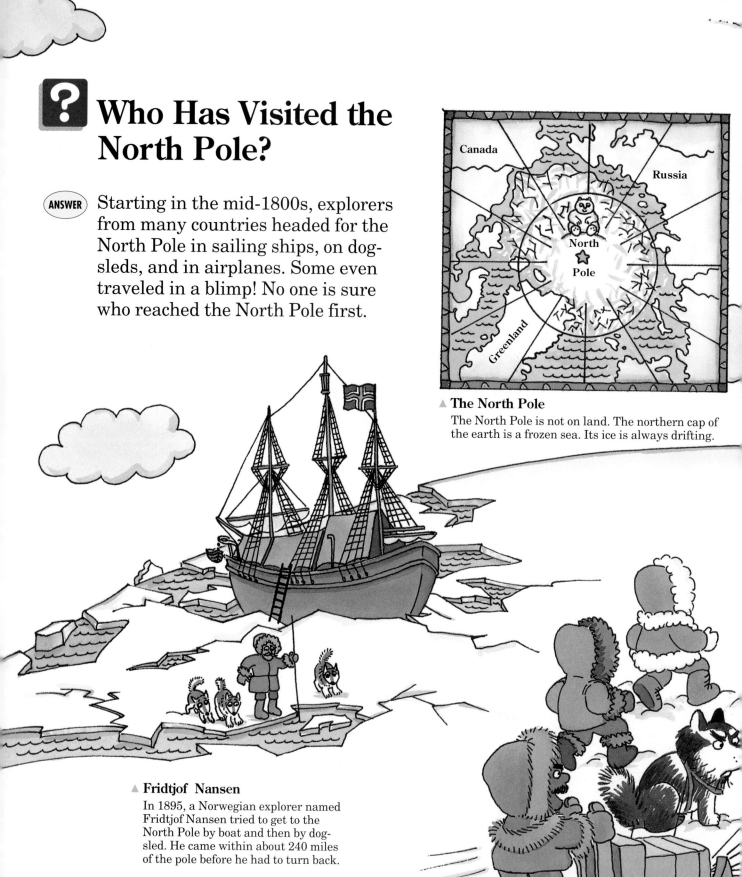

? Who Has Visited the North Pole?

ANSWER Starting in the mid-1800s, explorers from many countries headed for the North Pole in sailing ships, on dog-sleds, and in airplanes. Some even traveled in a blimp! No one is sure who reached the North Pole first.

Canada

Russia

North Pole

Greenland

▲ **The North Pole**

The North Pole is not on land. The northern cap of the earth is a frozen sea. Its ice is always drifting.

▲ **Fridtjof Nansen**

In 1895, a Norwegian explorer named Fridtjof Nansen tried to get to the North Pole by boat and then by dog-sled. He came within about 240 miles of the pole before he had to turn back.

▶ **Peary and Henson**

Americans Robert Peary and Matthew Henson, along with four Inuit explorers, set off for the North Pole by dogsled in 1909. Peary said that he and Henson reached the pole on April 5. Some people claim he never made it all the way there.

▲ Amundsen, Ellsworth, & Nobile

Norwegian Roald Amundsen,
American Lincoln Ellsworth,
and Italian Umberto Nobile flew
over the North Pole in a blimp
on May 12, 1926.

▲ Richard Byrd

Richard E. Byrd, an American explorer, said that he
and his pilot, Floyd Bennett,
flew over the North Pole in
an airplane on May 9, 1926.

North Pole

▲ Louise Boyd

Louise Arner Boyd was an
American explorer and polar-
bear hunter. She studied and
mapped many parts of Greenland in the 1920s.

● To the Parent

Arctic exploration has been—and
continues to be—difficult and dangerous. The drifting Arctic ice can
carry explorers far from their desti-
nation; fog and blizzards block
their path. To top it all off, early
navigational methods were crude
and inaccurate. As a result, no one
can say for certain who reached the
North Pole first. Both Peary's and
Byrd's claims have been disputed.

39

What Was the Race to the South Pole?

ANSWER In 1911, two men wanted to reach the South Pole first. One was Robert Scott, an Englishman. The other was Roald Amundsen, a Norwegian. They sailed to the pole at the same time and raced across the icy land. Amundsen's team got to the pole first. Scott and three others died in a blizzard on the way back.

▼ **A plan that failed**
Scott used ponies as well as dogs to pull his sleds, but the ponies soon died from the cold. Scott's men had to pull some of the sleds themselves.

◄ **A dogged success**
Roald Amundsen was well prepared for his journey. He used sled dogs to pull his loads.

The South Pole

The South Pole is 700 miles inland from the coast of Antarctica—the highest, driest, and windiest continent on Earth.

South Pole

"Had we lived, I would have had a tale to tell of the hardihood, endurance, and courage of my companions which would have stirred the heart of every English-man. These rough notes and our dead bodies must tell the tale."—from Robert Scott's last message, written in his tent with a blizzard howling outside

South

■ Norman Vaughan

In 1929, when Norman Vaughan was 23, he went to Antarctica with Admiral Richard Byrd. Byrd named a mountain after him. In 1994, just a few days before his 89th birthday, Vaughan returned to Antarctica and climbed "his" mountain for the first time.

? Which Places Were Never Discovered?

ANSWER For thousands of years, stories have told of lost cities of gold or faraway countries with strange monsters living in them. Sometimes people have gone looking for these made-up places. Even famous explorers have searched for imaginary lands.

■ A storybook city

People have searched for the lost kingdom of Atlantis for centuries. Stories say this rich land blew up in a volcanic eruption and sank beneath the waves.

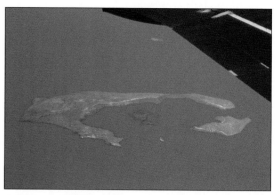

▲ **The real Atlantis?**
In 1500 BC, a volcano on the Mediterranean island of Thera exploded with a huge blast. Could this have started the story of Atlantis?

■ Prester John's kingdom

Travelers used to look for the Asian lands of King Prester John. Supposedly, this country had horned or one-eyed men, griffins, centaurs, giants—and jewels.

■ El Dorado

Some explorers searched for a man named El Dorado, who ruled a city of gold. He was said to be dusted with gold powder every morning.

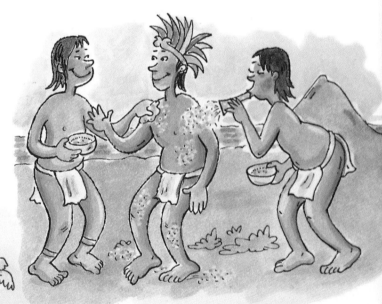

■ The Fountain of Youth

The Spaniard Juan Ponce de León explored Florida in the 1500s. Stories say he was looking for the mythical Fountain of Youth, which made people younger with just one drink.

● To the Parent

Nonexistent lands often grip the imagination more powerfully than real ones. To this day, people search for Atlantis, first mentioned by Plato around 355 BC. In many cases, the lure of these lost lands is a treasure in gold and jewels.

❓ Which Explorers Never Came Back?

ANSWER Explorers live dangerously. Seeking new lands, they face bad weather, deadly animals, sickness, and angry people. So it is not surprising that some explorers never returned from their travels. In fact, some seemed to vanish into thin air. To this day, no one knows what happened to these famous explorers.

■ John Cabot

In 1498, Italian explorer John Cabot sailed from England with four ships. He was looking for the island he called "Cipango," or Japan. Nothing more was ever heard of him or his ships.

■ Percy Fawcett

British engineer Percy Fawcett *(second from right)* and his fellow adventurers searched for the legendary "City X" in the jungles of Brazil. In 1925, the men disappeared. Some say their descendants still live in the jungle.

■ Saint-Exupéry

Antoine de Saint-Exupéry was a French writer and airplane pilot. His books often told of his adventures flying planes over the desert. His most famous book, *The Little Prince*, was the story of a boy who lives on a tiny planet. In 1944, during World War II, Saint-Exupéry flew out over the Mediterranean Sea. He was never seen again.

Amelia Earhart in her flight suit.

■ Amelia Earhart

Amelia Earhart was a famous pilot in the early days of airplanes. She was the first woman to fly across the Atlantic Ocean, and the first person to fly alone from Hawaii to California. In 1937, while Earhart was trying to fly around the world, her plane disappeared over the Pacific Ocean. No one knows what happened to her.

? Can People Explore by Bicycle?

ANSWER People can—and do—travel thousands of miles on bicycles. A bike lets you feel the weather, see the countryside, and meet the people of a new place. That's why some people say it's the only way to travel! Since the 19th century, adventurers have crossed many unlikely parts of the world on the seat of a bike.

■ Shift into your "grainy" gear!

In the late 1800s, Fanny Bullock Workman and her husband, Dr. William Workman, cycled across the Sahara Desert in Africa. They also pedaled thousands of miles from southern India to the Himalaya Mountains.

■ From Ireland to India on a bike

Dervla Murphy, an Irish girl, got an atlas and a bicycle for her 10th birthday. She decided she would ride her bike to India someday. In 1963, Murphy did it—even though she was chased by wolves on the way.

■ Laptops on wheels

Dan Buettner is a modern bicycle explorer. He has ridden across Siberia, Africa, and Central America. He often takes a computer with him and uses it to send messages to kids in school.

● To the Parent

Bicycle explorers have ranged from the intrepid Workmans, who pedaled wearing heavy Victorian clothing, to Dan Buettner, who carried a $33,000 satellite dish and used the Internet to notify schoolchildren of his discoveries.

47

How Is the Rain Forest Explored?

ANSWER Tropical rain forests grow in warm, rainy parts of the world. They are home to many different plants and animals. Most of the animals live way up in the "canopy," or treetops. Scientists have some clever ways to study the canopy.

Walkways

One way to get from tree to tree without damaging the rain forest is to build a soft, bouncy bridge called a walkway.

Ropes

Some scientists use a rope and pulley to hoist themselves up to the treetops.

Giant trees

150 ft.

Rain-forest trees can grow to be 150 feet high. That's five times as tall as a two-story house! The branches start near the top, where the sunlight is.

A blimp can lower a raft—which looks like an inflatable octopus—onto the canopy. Researchers walk on the raft.

Cranes

Students of the rain forest swing through the treetops on the long arms of construction cranes.

Scaffolding

Metal towers let scientists climb high into the trees.

■ Alexander von Humboldt

Alexander von Humboldt was a German naturalist. In 1799, he went to study the Amazon rain forest. While there, he said, "I very stupidly placed my foot on an electric eel." Ouch!

● To the Parent

Tropical rain forests cover less than 10 percent of Earth's land surface, yet they hold more than half of the planet's animal species. Because these forests are being cut down at a rate of about 55,000 square miles per year, scientists feel they are racing against time to study them. The more information researchers discover about the canopy, the more ways they can devise to save the rain forests.

How Do People Find Sunken Treasure?

ANSWER Sometimes people just stumble across treasure—coins or silver bars—washed up on a beach. Most of the time, though, they go looking for it. Some treasure hunters dive into the sea and look for shipwrecks. Others have tools that can find metal at the bottom of the ocean.

Ow! Some treasure found my toe!

■ The *Atocha*

In 1622, a violent hurricane sank the Spanish treasure ship *Nuestra Señora de Atocha* near Florida. In 1985, after searching for 19 years with special machines, treasure hunter Mel Fisher found the ship. Its art and gold coins are worth about $400 million.

What Other Ships Have Been Found?

Some shipwrecks are valued not for their treasure but for their history. The British ship *Bounty,* for example, was the scene of a famous mutiny. The luxury ocean liner *Titanic* was advertised to passengers as "unsinkable."

■ The *Bounty*

In 1789, sailors on the *Bounty* took over the ship and sailed it to Pitcairn Island in the Pacific. There they burned it. In 1957, photographer Luis Marsden found its remains on the floor of Pitcairn's bay.

■ The *Titanic*

In 1985, explorer Robert Ballard located the *Titanic* where it had been since 1912—two miles beneath the icy Atlantic. People cannot go that deep in diving suits, so Ballard and his crew used *Alvin,* a remotely controlled submarine, to find the famous shipwreck.

● **To the Parent**

Some shipwreck hunters are looking for the gold and silver of lost Spanish galleons. Others are archaeologists who want to recapture lost pieces of history. A few are both. As in the case of the *Atocha,* a successful treasure hunt can yield a huge payoff. These quests have therefore become big business, involving investors and computer modeling. Historians prefer that ancient wrecks be uncovered slowly by experts, and that their contents be donated to museums.

? Who Was "Lucky Lindy"?

ANSWER "Lucky Lindy" was the nickname of Charles Lindbergh, an American airplane pilot. In 1927, when airplanes were still small and dangerous to fly, Lindbergh became the first person to fly alone across the Atlantic Ocean without stopping. His route took him from New York to Paris, France. The flight lasted 33 ½ tiring hours.

▲ **The Spirit of St. Louis**
Lindbergh's plane, *The Spirit of St. Louis*, was built to be light. It weighed just 5,135 pounds.

Paris, here I come!
To save fuel, Lindbergh flew only 100 miles an hour. To avoid storm clouds, he flew just above the waves. Sometimes Lindbergh had to pull up suddenly to avoid crashing into icebergs or the masts of ships.

> Which way is Ireland?

▶ **Hello down there!**
After 27 hours in the air, Lindbergh wasn't sure where he was. But then he spotted some fishing boats. He flew down next to one and shouted out, "Which way is Ireland?" The fishermen were too surprised to answer.

■ The magic of flight

Harry Houdini, the famous magician, was fascinated by airplanes. In 1910, in three flights lasting a few minutes each, he became the first person to fly a plane in the skies over Australia.

Who Flew around the World on a Single Tank of Gas?

ANSWER The first people to fly around the world without stopping, using just one tank of fuel, were pilots Jeana Yeager and Dick Rutan. They did it in a light airplane that they built themselves. Dick Rutan called their world record "the last first thing" in flight.

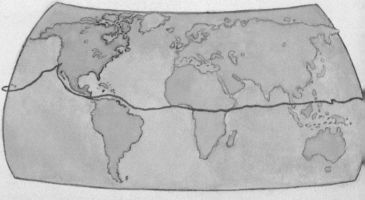

▲ **Around the world in nine days**
Rutan and Yeager's globe-circling flight began and ended in California in December 1986. Because the plane flew only 116 miles per hour, the two pilots needed nine days to cover 25,012 miles.

■ A gas tank with wings

The experimental plane, called *Voyager*, was made of layers of paper and graphite (graphite is also used as the "lead" in pencils). Its wings were wider than those of a 747, but *Voyager* was so light—less than one ton—that it didn't burn much fuel. *Voyager's* gas mileage was 23 times better than that of a jumbo jet.

■ No bathing, no standing

Voyager's cabin was only 7 ½ feet long and 3 ½ feet wide. It was not much bigger than a single human body, yet it had to hold two people. For nine days, Rutan and Yeager could not bathe or stand up. To change pilots, they rolled through the complicated maneuvers shown at right.

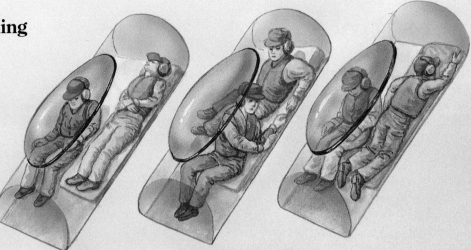

● **To the Parent**

The extraordinary experimental aircraft *Voyager* circled the world on 7,000 pounds of fuel. Buffeted by engine noise and turbulence, and with oxygen masks strapped to their faces, the two pilots had to stay awake almost continuously during the nine-day flight. When asked what part of the journey he liked best, Dick Rutan said, "I didn't enjoy any part of it."

Who Has Been to the Moon?

From 1969 to 1972, 12 men walked on the Moon. They flew there in seven different Apollo spacecraft. These astronauts wanted to show that it was possible to travel to other worlds. They also wanted to study the Moon. Even today, no one is sure where the Moon came from.

Are we there yet?

■ One giant leap

On July 20, 1969, Neil Armstrong became the first person to step on the Moon. Soon after, astronaut Buzz Aldrin *(right)* climbed down the lunar module's ladder. Their footprints *(above)* will not go away, because there is no wind on the Moon.

■ Space buggy

The Apollo astronauts traveled over the surface of the Moon in a specially built car called a lunar rover *(right)*. The astronauts collected lots of Moon rocks to study back on Earth.

■ A rock star from space

The rocks brought back from the Moon were very old. They showed that Earth and the Moon are about the same age—4.6 billion years.

> **TRY THIS**
>
> Hold up a ball about the size of a grapefruit. Now have a friend hold up a small ball the size of a Ping-Pong ball. Stand 12 ½ feet apart. This is how far apart Earth and the Moon would be if they were the size of these two balls.

● **To the Parent**

The first Apollo mission was a landmark in exploration, but most of the missions were devoted to geology. The astronauts collected hundreds of pounds of rocks in hopes of finding clues to the Moon's origin—whether it broke off from Earth, was captured by Earth, or formed in tandem with Earth. The rocks did not tell enough to answer the question.

Can Robots Go Exploring?

ANSWER Robots can explore places that are too dangerous for people, such as the inside of a volcano. The eight-legged robot known as *Dante*, shown at right, has cameras for eyes and a computer for a brain. It was built to crawl into smoking volcanoes and send back information on the lava and gases it finds inside.

■ Close encounter

Humans have never explored Saturn, but robots have. One of them, the deep-space probe *Voyager 2 (left)*, flew within 63,000 miles of Saturn in 1981. *Voyager 2* sent back 18,500 pictures of Saturn's rings and moons, then visited Uranus and Neptune. Next stop: the star Ross 248, which *Voyager 2* will reach in 40,000 years.

■ Undersea robots

How would you like to explore the ocean floor and never catch a cold? *Odyssey,* the eight-foot robot shown at left, does just that. It dives as deep as one mile to take pictures of undersea volcanoes and make sure pipelines are not leaking oil.

■ On the drawing board for tomorrow

▶ A spaced-out probe

Genghis the robot looks and acts like an ant: It has six legs and can move them one at a time. But don't look for it at your next picnic—this electronic insect is being designed to explore Mars!

▶ Calling Doctor Robot!

In the future, doctors may use a robot the size of a gnat to explore inside the human body and help people get well. The "microbot" would have a light, a camera, and movable arms. It would be tiny enough to swallow like a pill. Gulp!

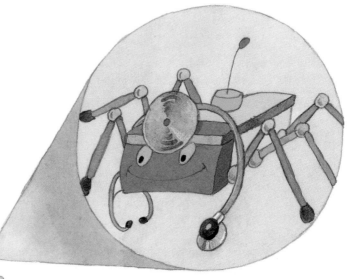

How Far Can You Fly a Balloon?

ANSWER The longest distance ever flown in a balloon is 5,768 miles. That's how far the four-man crew of *Double Eagle V* traveled in 1981, when they became the first balloonists to fly across the Pacific Ocean. Their helium balloon was 13 stories high. It lifted off from Nagashima, Japan, and touched down in the mountains of California nearly four days later.

■ Up, up, and away!

Double Eagle V soared calmly over Japan's Mount Fuji, but the rest of the ride was a "constant battle," said Captain Ben Abruzzo. The balloon was rocked by many storms.

What Is Big-Game Ballooning?

Floating along in a hot-air balloon is a good way to watch wild animals, also called big game. The animals don't seem to mind the balloon gliding overhead, and the passengers get a close-up look at the creatures below.

The first flight

In 1783, Jean-François Pilâtre de Rozier and the Marquis d'Arlandes floated over Paris in the first-ever manned balloon flight.

● **To the Parent**

Two French brothers, Joseph and Etienne Montgolfier, invented the hot-air balloon in 1783. Since then, balloonists have continually tried to set new records for time and distance flown. The most daring balloon feat of all—the circumnavigation of the globe—has been attempted by many adventurers, but none has come near completing the 25,000-mile journey.

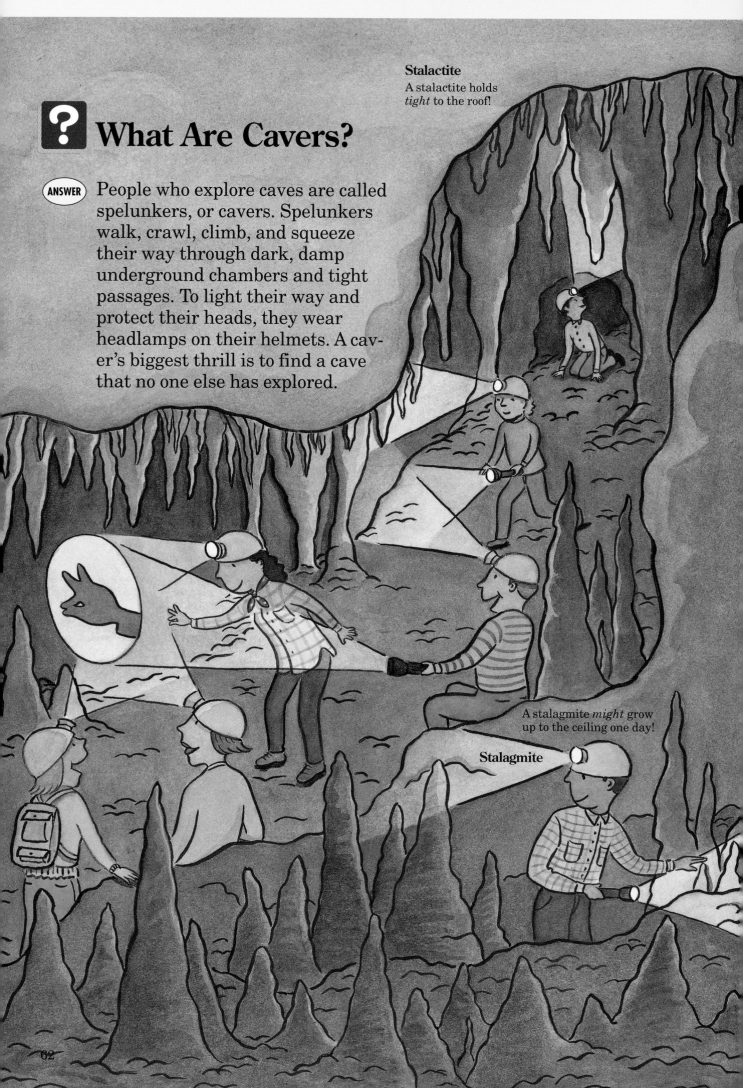

What Are Cavers?

ANSWER People who explore caves are called spelunkers, or cavers. Spelunkers walk, crawl, climb, and squeeze their way through dark, damp underground chambers and tight passages. To light their way and protect their heads, they wear headlamps on their helmets. A caver's biggest thrill is to find a cave that no one else has explored.

Stalactite
A stalactite holds *tight* to the roof!

A stalagmite *might* grow up to the ceiling one day!

Stalagmite

■ Diving in darkness

Underground streams flow through many caves. Sometimes a caver can paddle a boat or swim across the water. But if a passage is flooded, the only way to find out what lies at the other end is to dive through it. The cave diver at left is using a "rebreather," a piece of equipment that lets him stay underwater for 16 hours by recycling oxygen.

■ Underground art

In 1940, four boys were exploring a hill near Lascaux, France, when their dog disappeared. They followed its barking to a hole in the ground, crawled into it, and discovered cave walls covered with prehistoric paintings.

▲ The paintings in the Lascaux cavern are 17,000 years old.

63

Who Has Climbed the World's Highest Mountain?

ANSWER On May 29, 1953, Edmund Hillary and Tenzing Norgay (*right*) became the first people to reach the top of Mount Everest, 29,028 feet above sea level. Along the way, their oxygen lines froze up, and they had to scale a smooth, 40-foot-high wall of ice. Since then, more than 500 climbers have conquered the mighty peak—but 100 have died trying.

▲ Two mountain climbers in the first Canadian team to reach the top of Mount Everest perch high above the clouds in 1982.

What Is Free Climbing?

"Free climbers" crawl up steep slopes and rocky cliffs using only the climbing tools they were born with—their hands and feet. That makes the sport a very dangerous one. Some free climbers anchor themselves with safety ropes, which will catch them if they fall.

▲ Free climber Todd Skinner inches his way up El Capitan. Climbing down is just as challenging, says Skinner: "The adventure isn't over when you reach the top."

▼ Paul Piana reads in a sling hanging from El Capitan, a 3,000-foot-high California cliff. He slept like this 48 nights in a row—the time it took him to free-climb the peak.

■ This kid can climb!

Merrick Johnston started climbing mountains when she was five years old. In 1995, the 12-year-old became the youngest person to stand atop Alaska's 20,320-foot-high Mount McKinley, the tallest peak in North America.

? What Is an Aquanaut?

(ANSWER) An aquanaut is someone who explores the fascinating world below the surface of the sea. Aquanauts study the ocean floor, searching for natural resources. Sometimes they discover new plants or animals. Aquanaut Sylvia Earle, who began diving when she was 16 years old, has spent more than 6,000 hours exploring underwater.

■ Strolling in a deep-sea garden

Wearing a Jim suit and linked by cable to a small submarine, Sylvia Earle walked 1,250 feet deep in the Pacific Ocean in 1979. She saw spiraling bamboo coral, pink sea fans, and plumelike sea pens.

▼ The 1,000-pound Jim suit supplies divers with air. It also protects them from the crushing water pressure and freezing cold of the deep ocean.

Copper helmet

Gloves

Waterproof suit

Weighted boots

■ Hey! I can't move!

Deep-sea divers used to wear the heavy waterproof suit, gloves, boots, and copper helmet shown at left. This made it hard for them to move around underwater. An air hose to the surface supplied oxygen but limited how far the divers could go.

▲ Jacques Cousteau, master aquanaut

■ Scuba diving

Oceanographer Jacques Cousteau *(top)* helped invent scuba gear, shown above. With no air hoses to hold them back, scuba divers are free to explore as deep as 300 feet underwater.

● To the Parent

A scuba diver breathes air through a mouthpiece connected to a small oxygen tank carried on the back. (The word "scuba" stands for "self-contained underwater breathing apparatus.") Invented in 1943, scuba gear opened a new era of underwater exploration. Marine biologist Sylvia Earle pioneered using the new technology for ocean research.

? **What Was _Kon-Tiki_?**

ANSWER _Kon-Tiki_ was a raft made of balsa wood. It carried Norwegian explorer Thor Heyerdahl and five other men on a daring voyage across the Pacific Ocean in 1947. Heyerdahl believed that the islands of Polynesia were settled by people who sailed west from Peru many centuries ago. To prove that such a journey was possible, Heyerdahl built a balsa-wood raft and made the trip himself.

▲ **Thor Heyerdahl**

"We were riding on the wave back at breathless speed, our ramshackle craft creaking and groaning as she quivered under us. The excitement made one's blood boil."
—Thor Heyerdahl describing the voyage of _Kon-Tiki_

▲ **Building the raft**
Heyerdahl and his crew built _Kon-Tiki_ out of balsa-wood logs that they cut in the South American jungle. They tied the logs together with ropes of hemp to make a 40-foot raft, just as the ancient Peruvians might have done.

▲ **A fishy voyage**
Fish were so plentiful that they jumped onto _Kon-Tiki_ as it sailed. Each morning, the men collected the fish that had landed on deck during the night and cooked them for breakfast.

The pyramids and stone statues in Peru *(above)* look like those in Polynesia *(facing page)*. Heyerdahl saw this as a clue to the mystery of where the first Polynesians came from.

▲ A raft fit for a king

Thor Heyerdahl named his raft *Kon-Tiki* in honor of an ancient king of Peru. According to legend, Kon-Tiki left Peru a long time ago and sailed west across the ocean. Heyerdahl thought this story might be true, and that the king and his companions might have reached the islands of Polynesia. The face of Kon-Tiki was painted on the raft's sail.

▲ Land, ho!

The crew of *Kon-Tiki* braved raging storms, schools of sharks, and pods of whales. Finally, after 101 days at sea, they reached a tiny island in Polynesia. Heyerdahl had proved his theory.

● To the Parent

The voyage of *Kon-Tiki* covered about 4,300 miles. In 1970, Thor Heyerdahl undertook another epic sea voyage: He sailed from Morocco to Barbados in a papyrus reed boat named *Ra-2*, proving that ancient Egyptians could have used such vessels to cross the Atlantic Ocean and reach the New World.

? Who Has Looked for Monsters?

ANSWER Stories about monsters are told by people all over the world. Many scientists and adventurers have looked for proof that these mysterious creatures truly exist. The only one of these animals that has ever been found is the giant squid (dead ones have washed ashore). Scientists hope to find and film a giant squid soon, living in its deep-sea home.

▲ A giant squid from legend

▼ How giant is a giant squid?

The giant squid is not a made-up monster. It has eight arms and two tentacles, and each eye is bigger than your head. A giant squid can weigh one ton and grow 60 feet long—twice as long as a school bus. Inside its body are three hearts.

■ Have you seen us?

MISSING

▲ Mokele Mbembe

This fearsome beast is said to look like a dinosaur and live in swamps in Central Africa. People have reported seeing it for the last 200 years.

▲ Bigfoot

You can watch for this humanlike monster in remote woods of the northwest U.S., but don't expect to find it: Legends say that Bigfoot is quite shy.

▲ Mapinguari

People in Brazil's forests tell tales of a hairy beast that really stinks. Some say the smelly monster is actually the giant sloth, long thought to be extinct.

▲ The Loch Ness Monster

Many monster hunters have tried to find this huge animal that looks like a lizard. Nicknamed "Nessie," it is said to live in Loch Ness, a Scottish lake.

● To the Parent

The giant squid was considered a mythical beast until the 1870s, when several of the creatures beached in Newfoundland. Living about 3,000 feet deep in cold northern seas, the huge cephalopods are a favorite food of sperm whales. Giant squid rarely surface, but there have been occasional sightings of them—and even rare cases of boats being attacked. The search for giant squid and other hidden animals has launched a new science: cryptozoology.

Where Are the Ends of the Earth?

ANSWER It takes a lot of time and trouble to reach the actual ends of the earth— that is, the North and South Poles. People use the phrase "the ends of the earth" to describe any spot that is out of the way and hard to get to. You can visit some of them here!

◀ **Greenland icecap**
A sheet of ice two miles thick covers the interior of Greenland (which is white, not green!). No one lives there.

NORTH POLE

▲ **Takla Makan Desert**
This desert, in northwestern China, is one of the driest places on the planet. Its name means "Once you get in, you can never get out."

▼ **Tierra del Fuego**
A cluster of rocky, windswept islands at the tip of South America, Tierra del Fuego is home to many wild llamas— but not many people!

SOUTH POLE

▲ **Egypt's Western Desert**
Created by the wind, the sand dunes in this desert—part of Africa's Sahara—can grow to be 600 feet high and 100 miles long.

■ Alexandra David-Néel

"Ever since I was five years old," said Alexandra David-Néel, "I craved to go beyond the garden gate, to follow the road that passed it by, and to set out for the Unknown." When she grew up, the adventurous Frenchwoman explored much of Asia. In 1923, she entered the Himalayan kingdom of Tibet—a mysterious land that many people thought of as the end of the earth.

▼ To India by yak back
Alexandra David-Néel used any means of transport she could find to get where she wanted to go. In India, she rode through mountain passes on a yak.

▶ Across the Gobi by foot
To reach Tibet, David-Néel and her adopted son wandered through China's Gobi Desert for three years. Along the way, she found the source of the Po River.

Into Tibet in disguise
Lhasa, capital of Tibet, was off limits to foreigners. That didn't stop David-Néel. Disguised as a beggar *(left),* she slipped into the city in 1924.

● To the Parent
"Adventure is my only reason for living," declared Alexandra David-Néel, who lived to be 100. Born in 1868, the French opera singer moved to North Africa, then grew fascinated with Buddhism. She was the first Western woman to enter the forbidden city of Lhasa, the holy center of Tibetan Buddhism.

What Is Adventure Travel?

ANSWER Like the activities shown here, adventure travel is an exciting way to enjoy the great outdoors. Adventure travelers explore nature while learning new skills. Part of the adventure is discovering new things about yourself: You'll never know how far you can paddle a canoe or ride a horse until you try it!

Llama trekking

Horseback riding

Hiking

White-water rafting

Rock climbing

Mountain climbing

Snowshoeing

▼ Dogsledding

Canoeing

Tubing

Mountain biking

● **To the Parent**

Outdoor adventures should be age appropriate, but even very young children can hike on gentle trails or go along on canoe trips. Older children can attempt more strenuous challenges. Children and adults should wear proper safety equipment, including life jackets for water sports and helmets for biking and white-water rafting.

Who Has Been to the Most Places?

(ANSWER) American globetrotter John Clouse has visited more countries than anyone else. Clouse has set foot in all but six of the world's 257 nations, island groups, and other geographical regions. His son Chauncey, who often travels with his father, had visited 100 countries by the time he was five years old!

▲ For a visit to count toward the record of World's Most Traveled Man, Clouse had to touch his feet to the ground and get his passport stamped.

▼ **Around the world on foot**
With a mule to carry his gear, American David Kunst set off in 1970 to walk around the world. During the four-year trek, he covered 15,400 miles and wore out 21 pairs of shoes.

▼ **Around the world on wheels**
Canadian athlete Rick Hansen circled the globe in a wheelchair from 1985 to 1987. He went 25,000 miles, visited 34 countries, and collected $8 million for spinal-cord research.

Who Was the First Travel Writer?

Ida Pfeiffer was an average Austrian housewife in the early 1800s, but after her children grew up and left home she took off to see the world. Unlike most women in those days, Pfeiffer traveled by herself and lived with native peoples whenever she could. Pfeiffer circled the globe twice. She kept diaries of all her adventures *(below)* and turned them into popular travel books.

▼ A slow boat in China
In China, Ida Pfeiffer rode a cargo boat called a junk. In cities, she dressed as a man because a woman traveling alone was so unusual.

▲ Hunting adventure in India
Pfeiffer visited India on her first trip around the world. She lived with the villagers and joined them on tiger hunts in the jungle.

▼ Seeing the sights in Egypt
In Egypt, Ida Pfeiffer paid a visit to the sphinx—a stone figure with the head of a man and the body of a lion.

● To the Parent

Born in Vienna in 1797, Ida Pfeiffer had "an insatiable desire for travel." In Borneo, wearing trousers covered by a petticoat, she trudged through dense jungle to live with local tribespeople. Pfeiffer described the Dyak people, whose practice of ritual headhunting had earned them a fearsome reputation among Europeans, as "honest, good-natured, and modest."

❓ What Do I Need to Go Exploring?

(ANSWER) A curious mind is the only thing you *really* need to go exploring, but a few tools come in handy as well. Binoculars make things look closer; a magnifying glass makes them look bigger. A jour- nal lets you write down discov- eries; a sketchbook lets you draw them. You might also bring a box for rocks, a net for bugs (don't forget to let them go!), and a camera for memories.

What's Left to Find?

Many things and places have yet to be discovered. Earth's rain forests, for example, are thought to hold thousands of unknown life forms. One researcher found 1,500 types of beetle—many of them new to science—on a single tree in Panama. The seas hold untold treasures, too; less than one percent of the ocean bottom has been explored. A bit farther from home, astronomers have discovered two planets in our galaxy that might be able to support life. Can you imagine what it would be like to explore a whole new world?

■ From the riches of the rain forest...

■ ...to the secrets of the sea...

● **To the Parent**

Our solar system belongs to the Milky Way Galaxy, which teems with more than 100 billion stars. Many astronomers believe that at least some of those stars are orbited by Earthlike planets, which in turn may be inhabited by intelligent life forms. Astronomer Frank Drake, for one, has posited the existence of 10,000 advanced civilizations in the Milky Way.

...to deep space, wonders await!

Growing-Up Album

A-maze-ing Adventure

As you found out on pages 34-35, even explorers get lost. Can you help the five adventurers below get through the maze to reach the things that made them famous?

1. Marco Polo

2. Ibn Battuta

3. Astronaut

4. Pirate

5. Lewis & Clark

A. Timbuktu

B. Pacific Ocean

C. Treasure

D. China

E. Moon

Got a Match?

Without a way to travel, these seven explorers would
have stayed home—and this book would not exist! Try
to match each person to the vehicle he or she used.

3. Ben Abruzzo

1. Mary Kingsley

2. Robert Scott

A.

7
Chen
9407

B.

Charles
L. 5

C.

Ben
A. 3

4. Dervla Murphy

5. Charles Lindbergh

6. Leif Ericson

7. Cheng Ho

D. mary king 1

E. Robert Scott 2

F. Leif E. 6

G. Pervla M. 4

Answers: A-7; B-5; C-3; D-1; E-2; F-6; G-4.

85

Where Do They All Belong?

You probably know all the foods, animals, and objects shown here, but many of them were strange sights to the explorers who first saw them. Try to guess where on the map each item comes from.

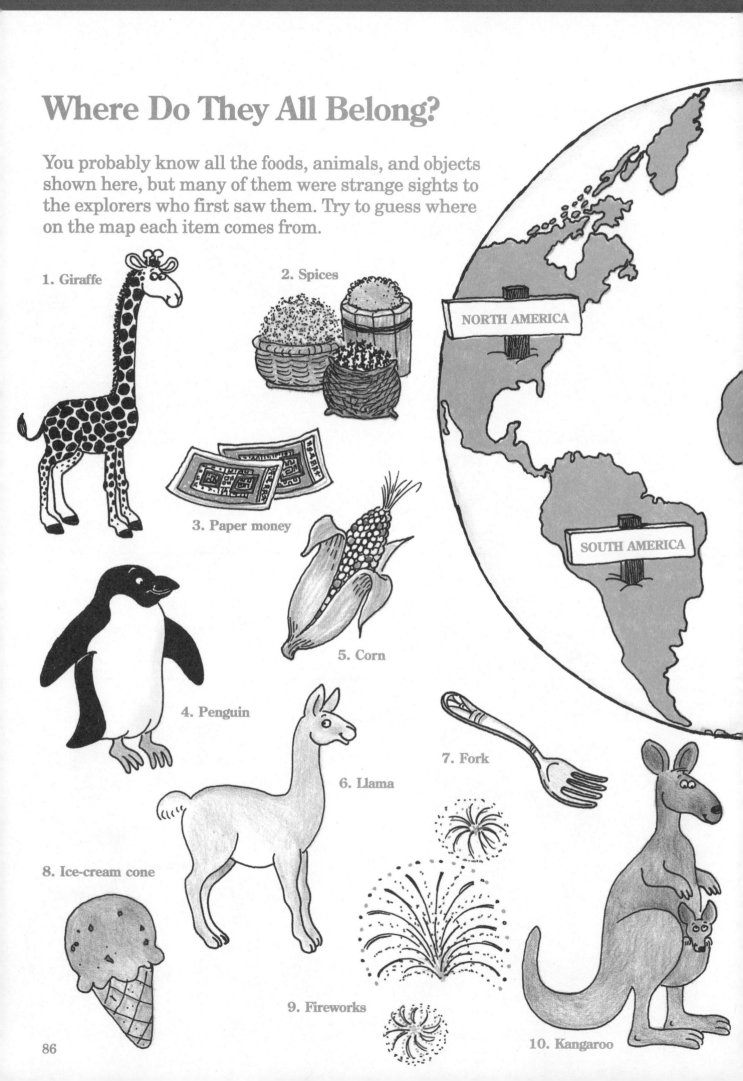

1. Giraffe

2. Spices

3. Paper money

4. Penguin

5. Corn

6. Llama

7. Fork

8. Ice-cream cone

9. Fireworks

10. Kangaroo

NORTH AMERICA

SOUTH AMERICA

11. Canoe

12. Potatoes and tomatoes

13. Koala

14. Printing

15. Coffee

16. Umbrella

17. Turkey

18. Magnifying glass

19. Chocolate

20. Polar bear

ARCTIC

EUROPE

ASIA

AFRICA

AUSTRALIA

ANTARCTICA

Answers: Asia–2, 3, 9, 14, 18; Europe–7, 16; Africa–1, 15; South America–6, 19; North America–5, 8, 11, 12, 17; the Arctic–20; Australia–10, 13; Antarctica–4.

TIME® LIFE BOOKS

Time-Life Books is a division of Time Life Inc.

TIME LIFE INC.

PRESIDENT and CEO: George Artandi

TIME-LIFE BOOKS

PRESIDENT: John D. Hall
PUBLISHER/MANAGING EDITOR: Neil Kagan

A Child's First Library of Learning
EXPLORERS & ADVENTURERS

EDITOR: Allan Fallow
DIRECTOR, NEW PRODUCT DEVELOPMENT: Elizabeth D. Ward
MARKETING DIRECTOR: Janine Wilkin

Deputy Editor: Terrell Smith
Picture Coordinator: David A. Herod
Picture Researcher: Mary M. Saxton

Design: Studio A—Antonio Alcalá, Sue Dowdall, Virginia Ibarra-Garza,
Wendy Schleicher, Melissa Wilets
Special Contributors: Pat Daniels, Marfé Ferguson Delano,
Jocelyn Lindsay (research and writing); Colette Stockum (copyedit).

Consultants: Melvin Marcus is a geography professor at Arizona State
University; Lawrence Millman, an expert in the history of exploration, is
a member of the Explorers Club in New York; Donald E. Vermeer is a research scholar in geography at California Polytechnic State University.

Correspondents: Maria Vincenza Aloisi (Paris), Christine Hinze
(London), Christina Lieberman (New York).

Vice President, Director of Finance: Christopher Hearing
Vice President, Book Production: Marjann Caldwell
Director of Operations: Eileen Bradley
Director of Photography and Research: John Conrad Weiser
Director of Editorial Administration: Barbara Levitt
Production Manager: Marlene Zack
Quality Assurance Manager: James King
Library: Louise D. Forstall

Photography: The sources for the photographs that appear in this book are
listed below. Credits from left to right are separated by semicolons; credits
from top to bottom are separated by dashes.
Cover: © Phillip and Karen Smith/Tony Stone Images. Back cover: Courtesy
of The Cayman Islands Department of Tourism. 1: © Dugald Bremner/Tony
Stone Images. 11: Jan Nauta/Photography Museum of New Zealand Te Papa
Tongarewa, B.018456. 17: James L. Stanfield/National Geographic Image Collection–Chris Johns/National Geographic Image Collection. 18: Science Mu-
seum/Science and Society Picture Library, London. 19: Copyright Oriental
and India Office Collections, British Library, London. 22: Cotton R. Coul-
son/National Geographic Image Collection. 25: Robin Graham/National Geographic Image Collection. 36: Liverpool Libraries and Information Service, Liverpool, England. 41: © Gordon Wiltsie/Alpenimage, Ltd. 42: © The Harold E.
Edgerton 1992 Trust, courtesy Palm Press, Inc. 44: MSI/Aldus Archive, London. 45: © John Phillips/Motovun Copublishers, Lucerne, Switzerland; illus-
tration from *The Little Prince* by Antoine de Saint-Exupéry, copyright 1943,
and renewed 1971 by Harcourt Brace & Company, reproduced by permission
of the publisher (North American Rights)/copyright: Antoine de Saint-Exupéry, 1996 (World Rights)–A.Y. Owen, Courtesy The 99s Inc., International
Women Pilots Organization, Oklahoma City. 51: Painting by Ken Marschall,
from *Discovery of the Titanic* © 1987 by Robert D. Ballard, a Madison Press
book. 52: The State Historical Society of Wisconsin, neg no. WHi (X3)45026.
53: From the Sidney H. Radner collection of the Houdini Historical Center, Ap-
pleton, Wisconsin. 56, 57: NASA, neg. nos. 69-HC-687; 69-HC-680; 70-HC-757;
71-HC-1140. 58: NASA/JPL. 60: *Tokyo Shimbun.* 63: Association La Venta, Tre-
viso, Italy/Roberto Rinaldi–Sisse Brimberg/National Geographic Image Collection. 64: Pat Morrow/First Light. 65: Bill Hatcher; Galen Rowell/Mountain
Light. 66: Reprinted with permission from Popular Science Magazines. ©
1995, Times Mirror Magazines Inc. 67: The Cousteau Society, Paris. 68: Photo:
Kon-Tiki Museum, Oslo, Norway. 70: The Granger Collection, New York. 72:
Clockwise from top left, Bill Glass/Root Resources; Dr. Georg Gerster (2);
James L. Stanfield/National Geographic Image Collection. 73: Fondation
Alexandra David-Néel. 80: © Frank Zullo. 81: JoAnn Simmons-Swing.

Illustrations: **Loel Barr:** 16-17, 28, 34 *(top)*, 36-37, 43 *(middle and bottom)*, 49
(bottom right), 50 *(top)*, 53, 56, 61, 63, 64, 70 *(top)*, 74-75. **Leila Cabib:** 46
(top), 47. **Annie Lunsford:** 19, 34 *(bottom)*, 35, 42, 43 *(top)*, 58-59. **Roz
Schanzer:** 4-5, 12-13, 20-21, 26-27, 32-33, 38-41, 68-69, 76-77, 82-87. **Carol
Schwartz:** 10-11, 18, 29, 44-45, 50 *(bottom)*, 51, 54-55, 66-67, 70 *(bottom)*, 71,
79. **Bethann Thornburgh:** 8-9, 22-23, 30-31, 46 *(bottom)*, 48-49 *(except bottom
right)*, 57, 62, 72, 78. **Bobbi Tull:** 6-7, 14-15, 24-25, 52, 65, 73.

First printing. Printed in U.S.A.
Published simultaneously in Canada.
School and library distribution by Time-Life Education, P.O. Box 85026,
Richmond, Virginia 23285-5026.

Time Life is a trademark of Time Warner Inc. U.S.A.

Library of Congress Cataloging in Publication Data
Explorers & Adventurers.
    88 pp.   1.4 cm.—(A child's first library of learning)
    Summary: Questions and answers present the achievements of his-
toric explorers and modern-day adventurers and explain such things as
why people were afraid to go south of the equator and how the early explorers traveled.
    ISBN 0-8094-9482-5
    1. Explorers—Juvenile literature. 2. Adventure and adventurers—Ju-
venile literature. [1. Explorers. 2. Adventure and adventurers. 3. Questions and answers.] I. Time-Life Books. II. Series.
G175.E95   1996
910'.922—dc20   96-38595
                                                            CIP
                                                            AC

OTHER PUBLICATIONS:

COOKING
Weight Watchers® Smart Choice
    Recipe Collection
Great Taste–Low Fat
Williams-Sonoma Kitchen Library

TIME-LIFE KIDS
Family Time Bible Stories
Library of First Questions and Answers
A Child's First Library of Learning
I Love Math
Nature Company Discoveries
Understanding Science & Nature

SCIENCE/NATURE
Voyage Through the Universe

DO IT YOURSELF
The Time-Life Complete Gardener
Home Repair and Improvement
The Art of Woodworking
Fix It Yourself

HISTORY
The American Story
Voices of the Civil War
The American Indians
Lost Civilizations
Mysteries of the Unknown
Time Frame
The Civil War
Cultural Atlas

For information on and a full description of any of the Time-Life Books
series listed above, please call 1-800-621-7026 or write:

Reader Information
Time-Life Customer Service
P.O. Box C-32068
Richmond, Virginia 23261-2068